THINGS THAT GO

PLANES EDITION

SPEEDY
PUBLISHING

Speedy Publishing LLC
40 E. Main St. #1156
Newark, DE 19711
www.speedypublishing.com

An airplane is a powered, fixed-wing aircraft that is propelled forward by thrust from a jet engine or propeller. They are used for transportation, recreation, research and military purposes.

The Wright brothers invented and flew the first airplane in 1903, , recognized as the first controlled, powered and sustained heavier-than-air human flight.

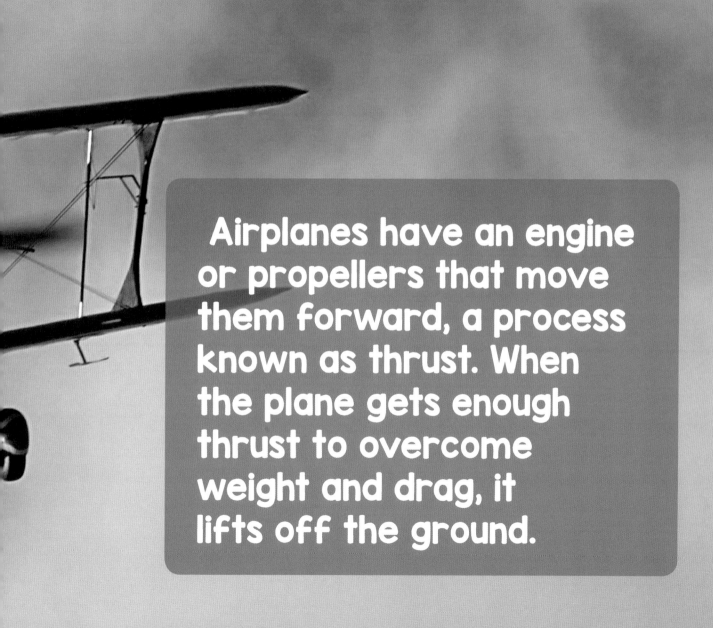

Airplanes have an engine or propellers that move them forward, a process known as thrust. When the plane gets enough thrust to overcome weight and drag, it lifts off the ground.

Smaller and older propeller planes make use of reciprocating engines to turn a propeller to create thrust.

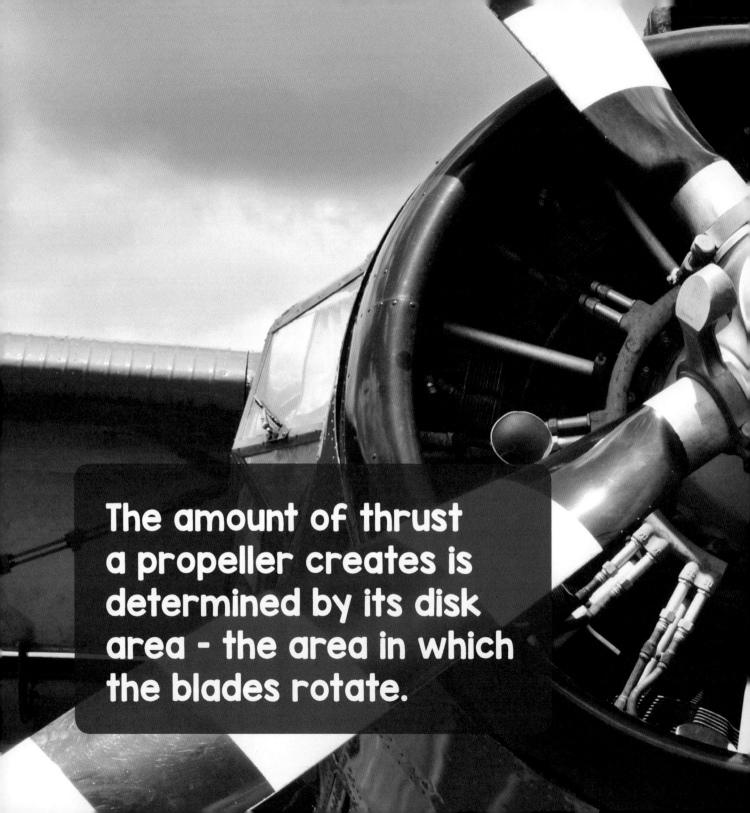

The amount of thrust a propeller creates is determined by its disk area - the area in which the blades rotate.

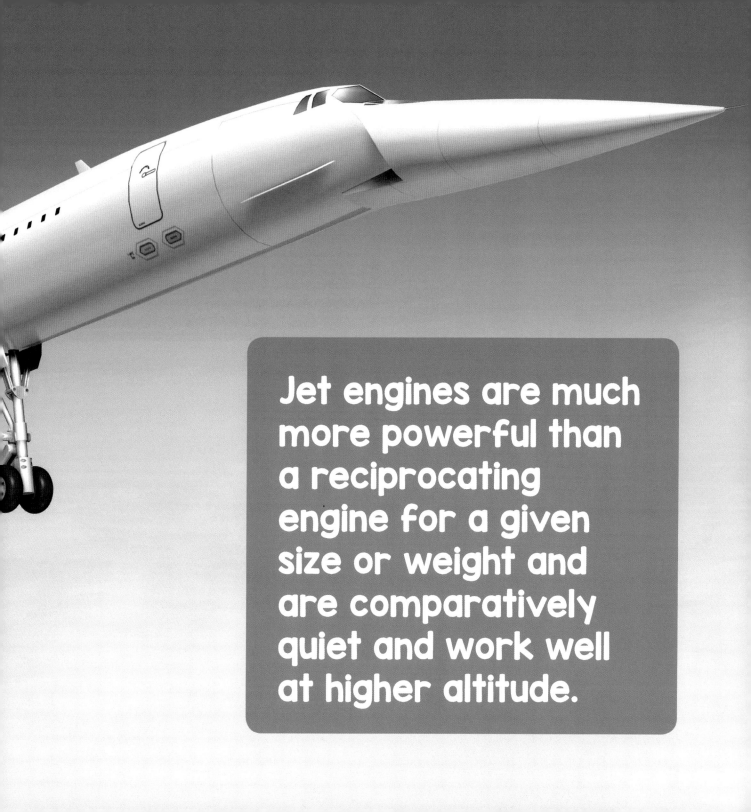

Jet engines are much more powerful than a reciprocating engine for a given size or weight and are comparatively quiet and work well at higher altitude.

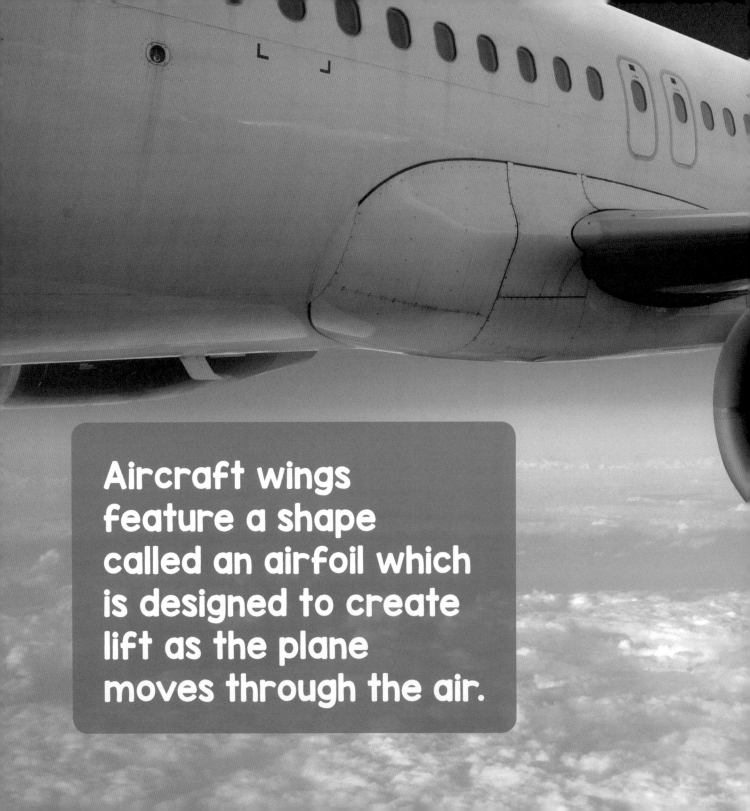

Aircraft wings feature a shape called an airfoil which is designed to create lift as the plane moves through the air.

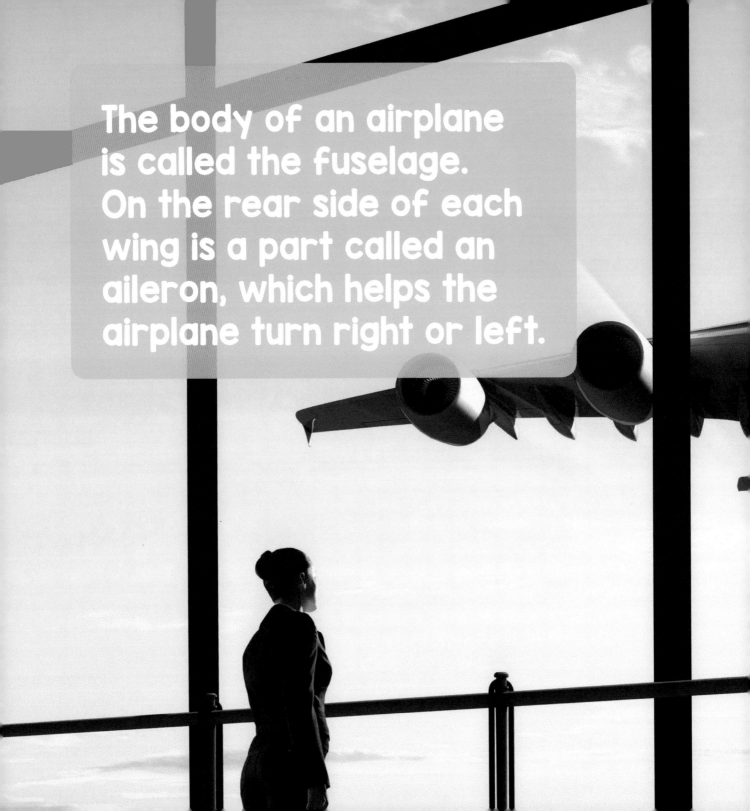

The body of an airplane is called the fuselage. On the rear side of each wing is a part called an aileron, which helps the airplane turn right or left.

Pilots usually control the plane from a cockpit located at the front of the fuselage.

Since the late 1930s, the monoplane has been the most common form for a fixed-wing aircraft.

One of the largest passenger airplane is the Boeing 747-400 and it can hold 524 passengers, not counting the crew.

Every day, there are approximately 200,000 flights around the world.

Most airplanes have a flight data recorder that keeps track of everything the plane does. These are often called "black boxes".

Each airline pilot flying the aircraft, eats a different meal to minimize the risk of all pilots on board being ill.

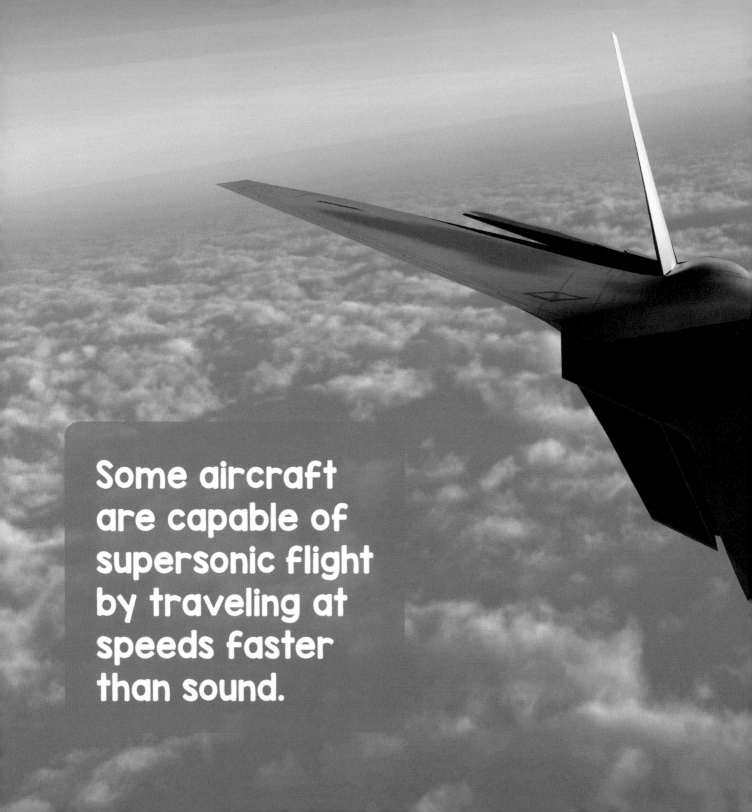

Some aircraft are capable of supersonic flight by traveling at speeds faster than sound.

Printed in Great Britain
by Amazon